8-bit is a form of digital art often referred to as pixel art.

All the illustrations in this book were created using 8-bit art and a 2 color palette at a resolution of 160 x 160. The title page was created using a 2 color palette at a resolution of 220 x 220. The cover art was created using a full color palette at a resolution of 220 x 220.

The font in this book is OCR-A. It was created for optical character recognition in 1968 and can be recognized by computers and humans. Used under license.

....

8-bit Kingdom
Copyright 2021 Joe Lacey

All rights reserved. Apart from any fair dealing for the purpose of private study, research, criticism or review, as permitted under the Copyright Designs and Patents Act, 1988, no part of this publication may be reproduced, stored in a retrieval system, or transmitted in any form or by any means, electronic, electrical, chemical, mechanical, optical, photocopying, recording or otherwise, without the prior written consent of the copyright owner. Enquiries should be addressed to the Publishers.

Joe Lacey has asserted his right under the Copyright, Designs and Patents Act, 1988, to be identified as the author of this book.

Published by Diner Mighty Graphics, publisher of humor and pop culture books. DinerMighty.com, Diner Mighty Graphics and the DM logo are trademarks of Diner Mighty.

ISBN: 978-1-7339842-7-0

....

"Never increase, beyond what is necessary, the number of entities required to explain anything."

- William of Ockham (1287-1347)

....

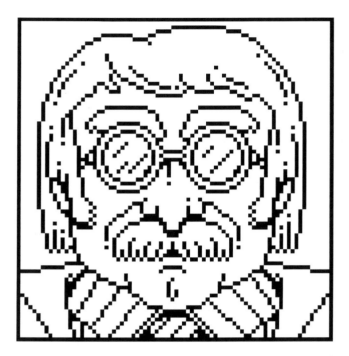

A MESSAGE FROM PROFESSOR PINCHUS PIXELTON of C. P. U.

In all my years of academia, studying and researching the ancient history of computer technology, there is only one moment in time that represents the quintessential computer experience - the fascinating yet often forgotten world of 8-bit Kingdom. To understand the modern-day computer world, it is imperative to start by studying the medieval tales of this land. It is here, in this world of magic and science that the modern computer age was born. For without the use of magic, there would be no science.

Before the *8-bit Book of Wisdom* was discovered in 1974, the origins of computing were lost in antiquity. Many of us, myself included, foolishly credited so-called computer "whiz kids", such as Charles Babbage, J. Presper Eckert and John Mauchly as the minds who brought us to the computer age. Today, we know this notion is sheer nonsense. Anyone in his right mind who reads the ancient text knows that it was King Octavious the Eighth of 8-Bit Kingdom who ushered in the modern computer age - over 1,200 years ago in the year 800 P.C. (Post Computers).

Although the *8-bit Book of Wisdom* does not fully explain all the circumstances involved in the development of the P.C. age, it does give us an understanding of how these events impacted not only the lives of the people then, but the lives of people now. We know King Octavious the Eighth battled the Malware Monarch, but we do not know any of the exact details. Despite this, one can easily see in the mind's eye how these battles played out with thanks to the illuminated manuscript. The illustrations contain information only hinted at or suggested in the narrative. It is up to the reader to complete the story.

The names, places, and events are also of extreme importance. The origins of computer programming terminology can be seen in the illustrations and the text. Also, many of our modern-day words were born in 8-bit Kingdom. A bit of Latin, a mixture of etymologies, and often an amalgamation of concepts are used to precisely define a person or an idea. For example, the name of the great monk Clavis Praestes is Latin for "Key Keeper".

As you read through this book, you will recognize familiar words that are common usage in personal computing. You will also come across many words that on the surface seem obscure, but rest assured the majority in this book have meaning rooted in computer technology. And remember, without the past, we have no future. Without the future, there is no meaning to the past.

....

- Professor Pinchus Pixelton
Professor Emeritus, Centralis Processui Universitas / C.P.U.

8-bit
BOOK of WISDOM

Existing since the dawn of time, the *8-bit Book of Wisdom* holds the infinite knowledge and history of 8-bit Kingdom. Its detailed maps recount the odyssey of early architects who built the North and South Bridges - connecting the many cities and hamlets of 8-bit Kingdom.

The cover is engraved with magical and cryptic symbols, protecting the vast knowledge within. Only a true 8-bit overseer can unlock its pages. In the wrong hands, the book could be used as a weapon to destroy all that is good!

The pages that follow are excerpts from this glorious treasure of knowledge!

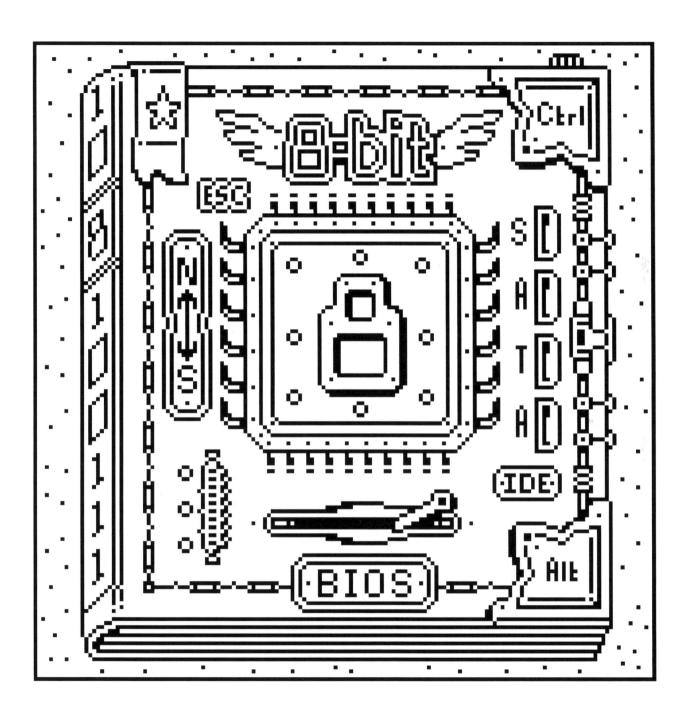

8-bit KINGDOM

Welcome to the magical world of 8-bit Kingdom where art and science are one and the same. Designed and built by King Octavious the Eighth, it is a marvel of architecture that stands as a symbol of all that is virtuous. Here, its people enjoy a life of intellect and play.

Its crystal clear ocean connects the kingdom to the sea of Erudition where knowledge flows to and fro. Even the clouds contain knowledge. Everywhere one looks, inspiration can be found. Peace has reigned for eight hundred years, but it is always in jeopardy if not watched over carefully and routinely.

KING OCTAVIOUS the Eighth

King Octavious the Eighth is the beloved ruler and architect of 8-bit Kingdom. He wears an eight-pronged crown encrusted with magical jewels. He keeps his kingdom clean and the fields well structured. The people of 8-bit Kingdom adore him. Every morning he surveys the land. He is very proud of his eight royal falcons who patrol the skies and alert the realms in the event of attacks from the evil Malwareia domain of the Malware Monarch.

Of our place in this world and our future in it, King Octavious proclaimed, "Wisdom is lost when technology becomes the leader of man." The king has spoken!

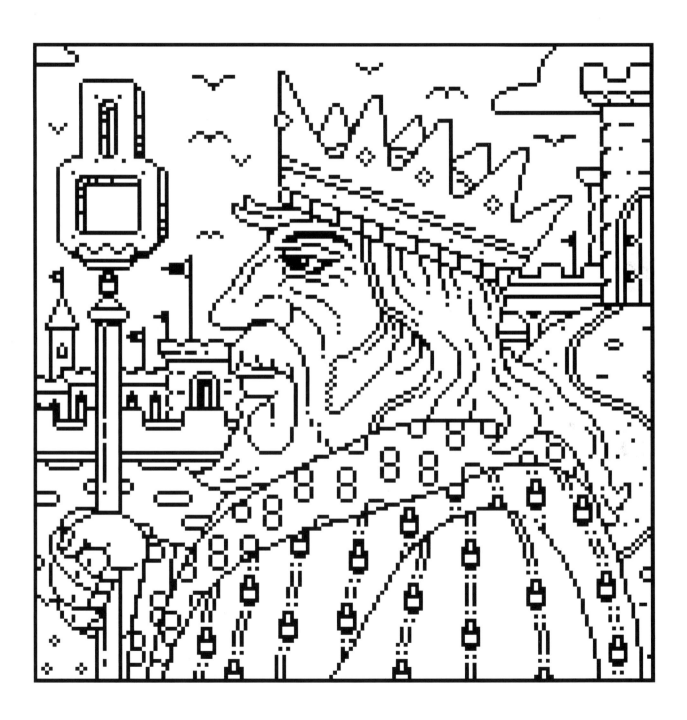

ROYAL CREST

Behold, the Royal Crest of Octavious the Eighth, King of 8-bit Kingdom! Its fierce dragon clutching the shield-like "8" symbolizes magic and wisdom. The royal crown is seen on the left. Eight royal falcons flank the dragon to the right. The dragon's wings symbolize freedom and the power of good.

Every wall in the kingdom is stamped with a magic knowledge seal known as a metal-oxide-transbitucilator. When one touches this seal it brings to life all the crests' dragons. When activated, these dragons protect the land and its people from the armies and monsters led by the evil Malware Monarch.

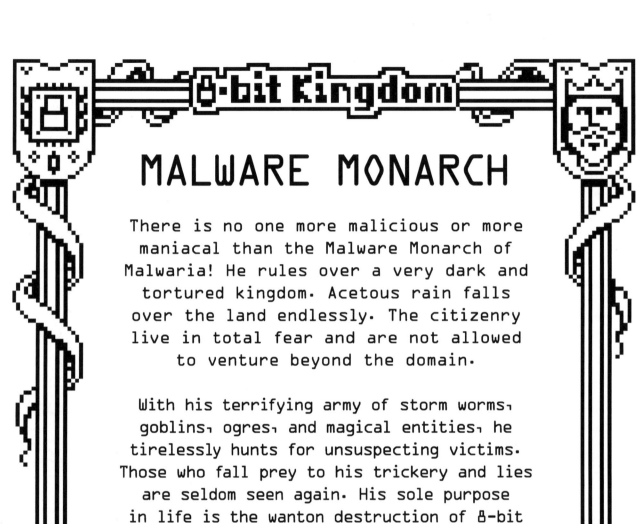

8-bit Kingdom

MALWARE MONARCH

There is no one more malicious or more maniacal than the Malware Monarch of Malwaria! He rules over a very dark and tortured kingdom. Acetous rain falls over the land endlessly. The citizenry live in total fear and are not allowed to venture beyond the domain.

With his terrifying army of storm worms, goblins, ogres, and magical entities, he tirelessly hunts for unsuspecting victims. Those who fall prey to his trickery and lies are seldom seen again. His sole purpose in life is the wanton destruction of 8-bit Kingdom! He will never cease this obsession until all are under his evil power.

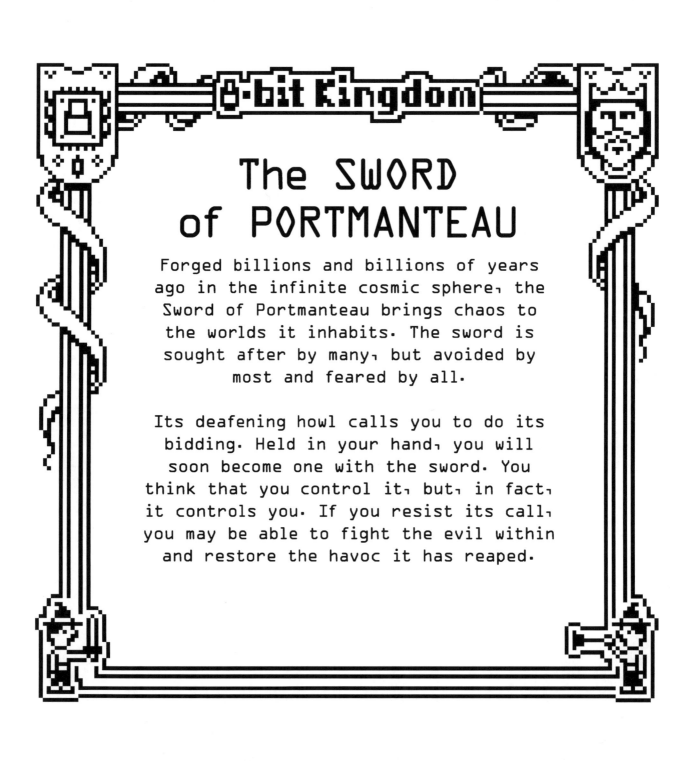

8-bit WIZARD

There is no one more powerful than an 8-bit wizard. But even they can have their powers impeded by magical beasts, sorcerers, and the ravages of time. Some are born 8-bit wizards while others find their calling later in life. There is no evidence that one wizard is greater or better than another wizard.

Wizards can summon creatures from the mist, control the minds of the weak, and affect the outcome of events. There are both noble and nefarious 8-bit wizards. Often, the two will engage in combat. If two 8-bit wizards combine powers, they can become unstoppable! Fortunately, this has never happened... yet.

8-bit Kingdom

SKY SERPENTS

The sky serpents emerge from the depths of 8-bit Kingdom as the onset of twilight envelops the land. They soar the heavens on mighty wings only during this brief time. They feast upon unsuspecting prey in ravenous attacks. Even the extreme cold of winter will not stop them from their eventide calling.

The serpents' only weakness is the bright light emanated from the staff of an 8-bit wizard. The power of this blinding force is summoned by the wizard when he utters the words: "Luminus Envelopetus Dragonatium!" It is brought forth from the dazzling celestial LED universe, a mystical dimension of great power and mystery.

8-bit Kingdom

QUEEN QUATROVIER

The beautiful Queen Quatrovier, along with her husband King Octavious the Eighth, rules the luminous land of 8-bit Kingdom and all its realms. The citizenry adores her just as much as they adore her husband. Through her regal actions, she inspires everyone in the kingdom to achieve greatness and strive for nothing less than perfection in all things large and small. She is beyond reproach.

Among the many duties to her land, nothing pleases her more than to care for the royal hounds. So regal are these magnificent creatures that they sport golden crowns and sleep on feathered mattresses with silken sheets.

 KINGDOM MAP

8-bit Kingdom is both a peaceful and dangerous place. The Faerie Caves and Elf regions are beautiful and inviting. Its rivers and oceans are home to many magical creatures. But heed this map before you journey onward! You do not want to be captured in Troll Swamp or lost in the Forest of Denial.

Eight moons rise above the land. The South bridge is a path for visitors. The North bridge is guarded at all times by King Octavious's army. It is the only way in or out of the Mirror Mountain, the gateway to uncharted lands of Malwaria. For no one who has entered Malwaria has ever returned... the same!

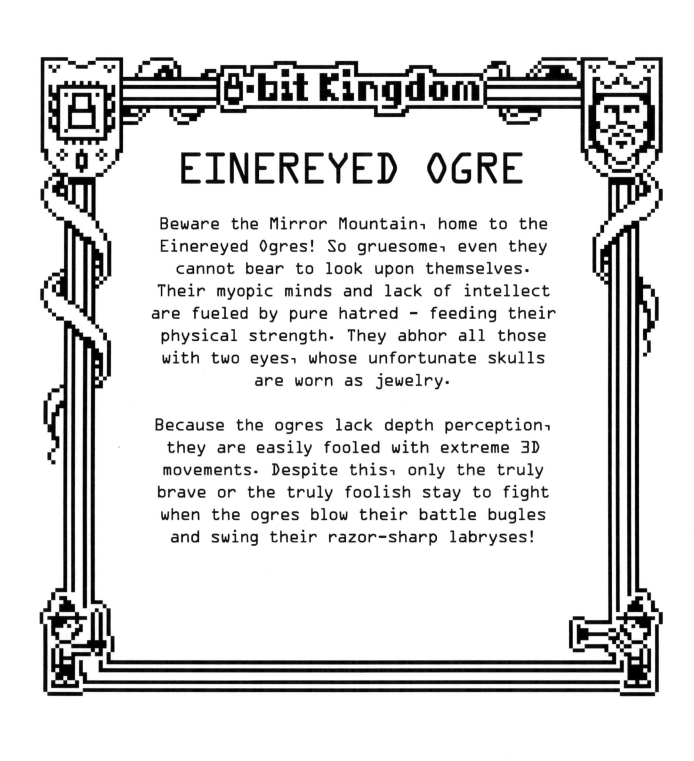

8-bit Kingdom

STORM WORMS

For centuries storm worms were small, harmless creatures. They lived beneath the earth, feeding upon lethal insects and disease-carrying vermin harmful to the inhabitants above the fertile land.

The Malware Monarch fiendishly uses his enchanted worm staff to turn the storm worms into giant monsters for his malice upon 8-bit Kingdom. A storm worm attack is often undetected until it is far too late. Lightning fills the skies, cities crumble, and the terrain cracks under the worms' colossal weight. Only a storm worm captured and retrained can be used in battle to defeat another storm worm.

8-bit Kingdom

FAERIES

Deep in secluded caves, faeries dwell in vast numbers. They typically come out at night, but can also be seen during the day. They often co-mingle with sprites, enticing them to create mischief while the faeries innocently watch. A faerie queen is just one of many kings and queens who rule the faerie lands.

It is said that to capture a faerie and gaze into its wings, one will see his future or his past, he knows not which. It is the faerie who controls the visions in his mind. This is why one should never cross a faerie, for they can be quite spiteful creatures!

SPRITES

Sprites are tiny creatures who live in very communal families. Often thought to be figments of the imagination, sprites will appear and disappear within the wink of an eye. They float in the ether of time and space and often cause mischief by moving objects. Though not purposely destructive, their pranks have been known to cause great damage.

When loud groups of five or more sprites suddenly appear it is best to distract them with shiny objects or serene music. This will cause them to fall asleep and return to their natural habitat. But make sure you leave the shiny objects out for at least a fortnight, lest the sprites return within moments of leaving.

8-bit Kingdom

TROLLS

Trolls are large creatures, but they should never be confused with giants. Trolls are just as dangerous as giants but with enormous heads, huge ears, and floppy feet. Trolls are slow-witted and prosaic by nature, while giants are quite clever and well-dressed.

Trolls busily bake cookies made from people captured in the Forest of Denial. All day and night they bake and pile cookies everywhere. Their smelly, half-eaten, stale concoctions can be found in obtrusive heaps, never to be cleaned up.

WARNING! Never enter the house of a troll lest ye be turned into a troll house cookie!

8-bit Kingdom

LATTER O'RISO LACH

There has never been a funnier or more inventive court jester than the famous Latter O'Riso Lach. Known as L.O.L., he wears these initials on a sash draped over his shoulder along with his 8-bit medal for laughing in the face of danger.

His many jokes incorporate magic and physical humor. He will pretend to be the wizard Wysiwyg and perform sleight of hand tricks, proving that "what you see is not what you get". He will leap and shout silly made-up words in an act he calls "acronymatics". He uses props in his comedy - small hand-painted caricatures known as imo'gees. L.O.L. is regarded as the funniest man in the universe.

ROYAL FALCONS

Soaring effortlessly through the vast firmament of 8-bit Kingdom, the eight royal falcons monitor its lands, skies, and seas. King Octavious is so proud of his troupe, he has decreed them to be of the highest noble order. The falcons' never-ending vigilance and heroism in the safeguarding of 8-bit Kingdom can never be dismissed.

The royal falcons are represented with two crests - an open claw and a bird in flight. Avis, the lead falcon, wears a gold 8-bit medallion which serves as a conveyance relay between his cast and the soldiery below. Only members of the royal family can possess falcon feathers.

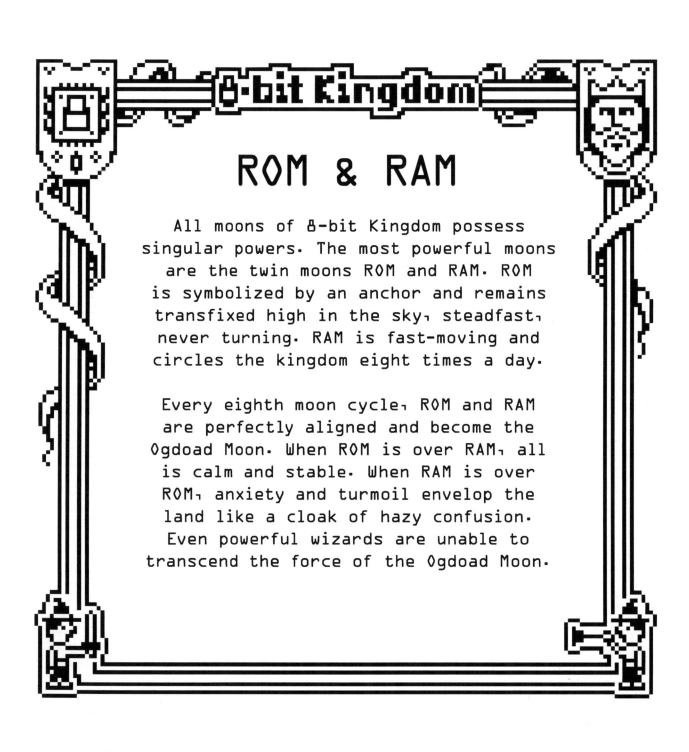

8-bit Kingdom

ROM & RAM

All moons of 8-bit Kingdom possess singular powers. The most powerful moons are the twin moons ROM and RAM. ROM is symbolized by an anchor and remains transfixed high in the sky, steadfast, never turning. RAM is fast-moving and circles the kingdom eight times a day.

Every eighth moon cycle, ROM and RAM are perfectly aligned and become the Ogdoad Moon. When ROM is over RAM, all is calm and stable. When RAM is over ROM, anxiety and turmoil envelop the land like a cloak of hazy confusion. Even powerful wizards are unable to transcend the force of the Ogdoad Moon.

8-bit Kingdom

TEKNCAL SEA PORT

The Tekncal Sea Port is the busiest and heaviest traveled maritime port of 8-bit Kingdom. Here, trade and commerce take place. Ships and boats from all over the world line up at the mouth of the port's man-made canal to enter and dock in its harbor. Tekncal Sea Port representatives guide the visitors in and assign them docking numbers. The wait is often long and tedious. Many leave in frustration.

The only threats to the Tekncal Sea Port are the frequent and brutal attacks by ginormous krakens, angry sea serpents, and of course, the Malware Monarch. During these attacks, the Tekncal Sea Port is unavailable for service.

CLAVIS PRAESTES

The order of monks known as the Volumen live in the great Tome Tower located on the outskirts of 8-bit Kingdom. Under the supervision of monk Clavis Praestes, they protect and study the ancient *Book of 8-bit Wisdom* and the magical silver disks of destiny.

These sacred artifacts are kept secure from enemies behind extremely thick stone barriers called firewalls and marked with shields depicting a broken sword. Only Clavis Praestes has free access to the library. Using a complex series of keys strung from a keychain draped over his shoulders, he conducts daily and nightly rounds, ensuring the eternal safety of the library.

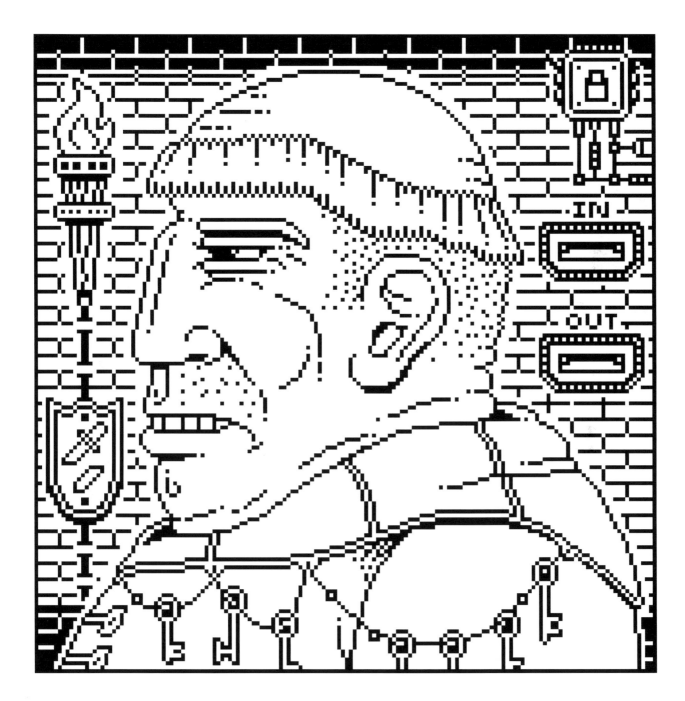

QUEEN NIMDA

Queen Nimda is an evil sorceress who will stop at nothing to destroy 8-bit Kingdom. Her spells are virtually unbreakable, but some have been able to fend themselves from her powerful attacks. She will often recite poetry before casting her spells:

Personality gone!
Free thee never!
From night to dawn!
Stuck forever!

She travels in a carriage drawn by two cloned elk. She believes in only one trusted creature, so when she finds one, she turns it into two, three, four... or four hundred! Her 500-man army is made from one cloned warrior.

8-bit Kingdom

SIR VERR

Known as the Knight who never sleeps, Sir Verr is ever vigilant and pure. This brave and valiant warrior resides in the floating city of Eethair. There, he looks over and serves all eight realms of 8-bit Kingdom. He cannot be swayed from his duty to man or country.

Many years ago the charismatic yet evil sorceress Queen Nimda cursed Sir Verr with the inability to sleep. Intended to torment his ever-waking life, this curse turned into an attribute. With his mighty suzerain of knights, Sir Verr stands ready to defend the defenseless, help the helpless, and march to battle against the vile Malware Monarch.

8-bit Kingdom

OOMPH

Oomph, also known as the "Dragon" or "Power Moon", supplies all the moons of 8-bit Kingdom with galactic energy. This energy is what gives each moon a unique aura. It circles 8-bit Kingdom 1,621 times a year and glows strong night and day. It is truly a sight to behold!

The Oomph Moon's symbol is an open ring with a vertical line through its top opening. Some have speculated that it represents a dragon's wings and a spire of fire. However, the ancient scrolls imply that it is a broken "8" serving as a gateway connecting this universe to its mirrored opposite. It is definitely a moon to be respected.

HACKING TOOLS

The Malware Monarch enlists many types of evildoers to help in his quest to conquer 8-bit Kingdom. One of the most dangerous is the hacker, since a hacker can be almost anyone. Often, the hacker thinks he is just being mischievous, but he is really being manipulated to perform the Malware Monarch's evil bidding.

Many tools are used by hackers to deface 8-bit Kingdom. Axes, maces, and swords are the weapons of choice for the more violent hacker. The more subtle hacker uses smaller tools such as hammers, screwdrivers, tongs, and even paper clips to pry off the magic knowledge seals that are embedded in the walls of 8-bit Kingdom.

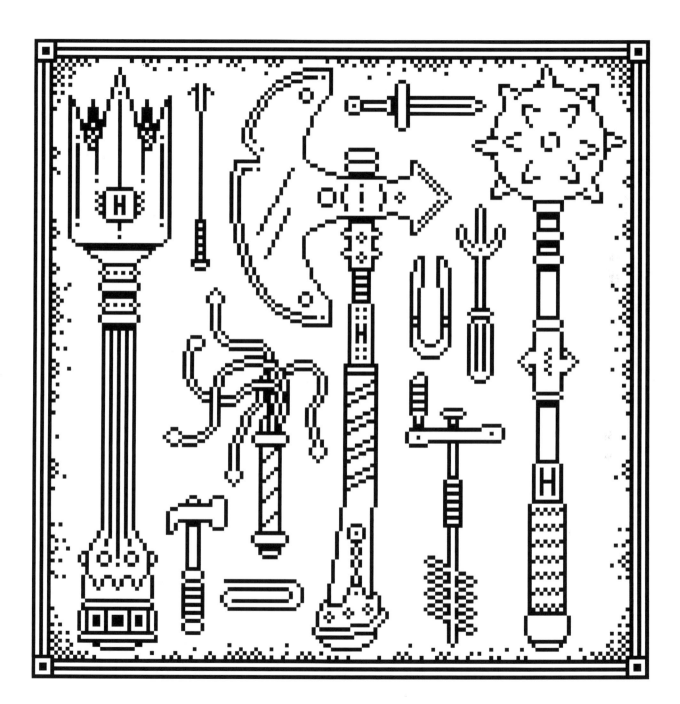

MONITAUR

The Monitaur, an enormous structure built before the beginning of time, watches over all of 8-bit Kingdom and its realms. No one knows why it was built or exactly what it does. Positioned ominously along the shore of the sea known as the Liquid Crystal Deep, its ever-present and unblinking eye rotates atop a mighty tower.

Some speculate the tower houses all the knowledge of the universe. Others feel it is a control system that regulates the tides of the ocean and the clouds in the sky. Hackers sail the LCD under cover of night, attempting to break in to the tower. As of this writing, no hacker has ever penetrated the tower's mighty defense systems.

DEATH

Death emerges from a glowing portal of blinding blue light. He is neither cruel nor pleasant. He simply exists. Death carries with him many objects that will predict a person's fate - a dead key, a bomb, a sickle, a mind-reading rat - but nothing as powerful as his hourglass of fortune (or misfortune).

His voice echoes as it shakes the land, warning the unfortunate victim "Halt, or catch fire!" Those who run or panic may succumb to his dominance. Those who keep a steady head as he turns his hourglass may live to see him another day. If the sands run down, your time is over. If the sands run up, your time continues and he leaves as quickly as he came.

8-bit Kingdom

OCTOCORN

The octocorns of 8-bit Kingdom appear when all eight moons of Ogdoad shine in the nighttime sky. Often mistaken for a unicorn, an octocorn has not one, but eight magical horns protruding from its forehead. As legend has it, an octocorn will protect and guide lost travelers by projecting a sparkling beam of light from its largest horn toward safety.

By decree of King Octavious the Eighth, it is prohibited to capture or abuse an octocorn. Only those with pure hubris would attempt such a foolish endeavor, for to do so would mean exile to the Forest of Denial.

RIME

Rime is the largest and fourth moon of 8-bit Kingdom. Known as the "ice moon", Rime brings frigid weather in the form of frost, ice, and snow. Rime is symbolized by two large opposing ice picks above and below its glowing rings. During the eighth cycle of Gelid, the time of darkness, Rime blocks the sun with inky clouds.

The coming of Rime is preceded by a cold misty fog that covers the land until only the highest mountain peaks are visible. Rime rotates on multiple gyroscopic axes. It is this unique rapid spinning that is believed to create the cooling winds that bring winter with its snows that fall upon the lands and hills.

8-bit Kingdom

CIRF ISLAND

Cirf Island is home to King Frank Eee and Queen Ay Net. The people of Cirf make materfamilias boards used in the construction of 8-bit Kingdom's walls. They also hand carve keyboards to hold the keys used in dungeons. Extra long keyboards are referred to as extended keyboards and are custom made for use at Tome Tower.

The island is located exactly north of 8-bit Kingdom. When one asks "Where is Cirf Island?", the reply is always "Cirf's up." Ships sail to and from the island delivering boards and exotic fruits. The island has no apples, but it does have pineapples.

THE CRAWLER

Beware the Crawler! It is a gargantuan extraterrestrial monster that roams the universe in search of planets to devour. This spider-like beast shoots sticky fiber strands from its body into the vastness of space. The strands float until they reach a planet or moon to envelop. When enough strands have joined they create a world wide web. The Crawler then appears from above with its eight eyes scanning the planet and cataloging all that is known of the inhabitants. Once finished, the Crawler consumes the entire planet. If it finds a planet to be too similar to one it has already destroyed, it ignores it and returns to hyperspace. Fortunately, the Crawler is merely an 8-bit legend.

8-bit Kingdom

PRINCE BANDWIDTH

Prince Bandwidth is a powerful Elfin warrior. Every citizen of 8-bit Kingdom is in awe of his stunning good looks and his impeccable style. Well versed in great literature, the fine arts, and all culinary delights, Prince Bandwidth is more than just a pretty face.

With his magic Mosfet sword, Prince Bandwidth keeps the roads and pathways in and out of 8-bit Kingdom free from intrusive web vines that are grown by the Malware Monarch. Web vines are not a great threat, but they are a nuisance and will slow down those who have to traverse any great distances.

8-bit Kingdom

ROYAL HOUNDS

All the people of 8-bit Kingdom revere Queen Quatrovier's eight Royal Hounds. More than companions, they possess great knowledge and help guard the Royal Tower.

The Royal Hounds have developed a unique language called Bork. It is similar to human speech in many ways. The dogs will append diminutive suffixes - "o" or an "er" to the end of words. A "br", "fr", or "mr" is added to the beginning of words, often replacing the first letter.

Brime frungry! Wanter foodo!
(I'm hungry! Want food!)

Bork uses only one punctuation mark - the exclamation point!

PRINCESS DOS

Princess Dos is the eighth daughter of King Octavious the Eighth and Queen Quatrovier. Her head is adorned with a glowing crown, long dangling earrings, and two gemstones depicting the moons Puretos and Loomen. Her throne is meticulously inlaid with multi-colored kernels taken from the mystic fields of Cee Drivia. Her two pet gargoyles sit and guard her.

Princess Dos is entrusted with updating the daily proceedings of 8-bit Kingdom. With the blinding light and heat emitted from her gemstones, she burns all of this information to silver disks of destiny. The disks float and spin above the main frame of her throne and are then stored in the great Tome Tower.

BUGABOOS

Bugaboos are an aggravation to all of 8-bit Kingdom. Even Malwaria is plagued by these pests. If the problem of these bugs is addressed early on, there is seldom any great threat. However, if left to thrive, a bugaboo can grow to tremendous size and cause great damage.

Much training has been implemented to slaying these hideous monsters. Special elite groups of 8-bit warriors known as Debuggers spend tireless days and nights eliminating smaller bugaboos and battling giant bugaboos. Nothing can stop bugaboo eggs falling from the sky during the eighth cycle of Puretos. Once embedded in the ground, the eggs hatch in eight days and baby bugaboos begin feeding immediately.

GOBLINS

Goblins have been a problem in 8-bit Kingdom for as long as there have been goblins. They live in small recesses of hollow trees. The trees are encrusted with fungus and mold for the goblins to eat. When night has fallen, they emerge from their holes and go to villages to steal gold, jewels, and anything they think appears valuable.

Most goblins have no redeeming qualities, other than their love of mice. Mice are attracted to a goblin's foul stench. You will often see a goblin with a pet mouse tethered to a wire. A wireless mouse or two often assist goblins in stealing the magic knowledge seals that are embedded in the walls of 8-bit Kingdom.

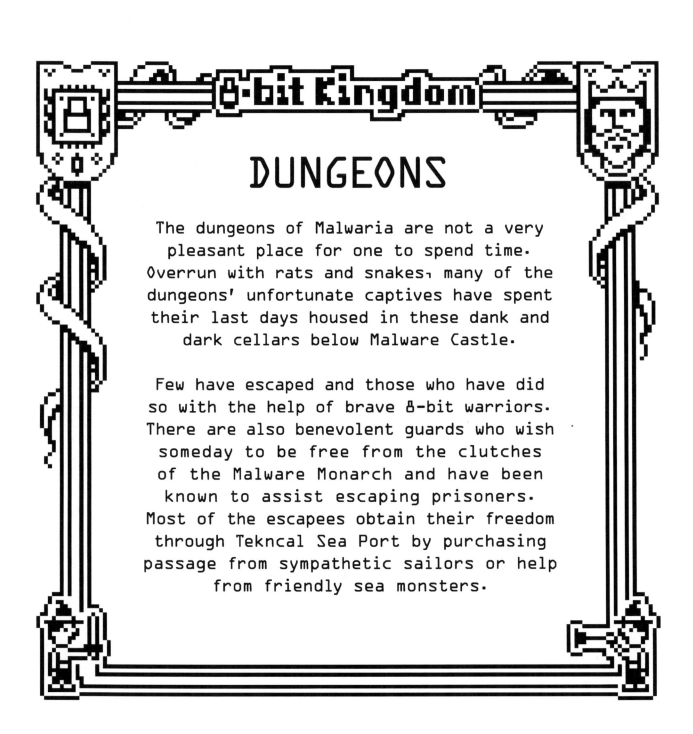

8-bit Kingdom

DUNGEONS

The dungeons of Malwaria are not a very pleasant place for one to spend time. Overrun with rats and snakes, many of the dungeons' unfortunate captives have spent their last days housed in these dank and dark cellars below Malware Castle.

Few have escaped and those who have did so with the help of brave 8-bit warriors. There are also benevolent guards who wish someday to be free from the clutches of the Malware Monarch and have been known to assist escaping prisoners. Most of the escapees obtain their freedom through Tekncal Sea Port by purchasing passage from sympathetic sailors or help from friendly sea monsters.

8-bit Kingdom

THE PROCESSOR

Every dungeon, be it in 8-bit Kingdom or in Malwaria, has a number of processors who oversee all prisoners. The Central Processor is in charge of controlling the input and output of prisoners, while other processors specialize in day-to-day activities and events.

The unlucky victims are placed in cells, and the bars are literally soldered shut by the processor. The cells are stacked upon each other in seemingly endless barred towers, their residents' new home for all eternity. Some lucky prisoners have escaped from these dungeons with outside help. These escapes are known as raids.

8-bit Kingdom

TROJAN HORSE

Using one of the Malware Monarch's own deceptions, King Octavious famously sent a large wooden horse to the doors of the Malware Castle. Perceived as a gift, the horse was pulled inside the gates by the guards. The foolish Malwarians celebrated their latest acquisition throughout the day.

As the Malwarians slept, King Octavious's plan became a reality. Under cover of a cloudy night, while the bats flew and the wolves howled at the moon, 88 brave 8-bit warriors hidden inside the equestrian contraption exited with swords drawn. They took the guards by surprise, and this long and bloody battle stopped the evil Malware Monarch's latest attack.

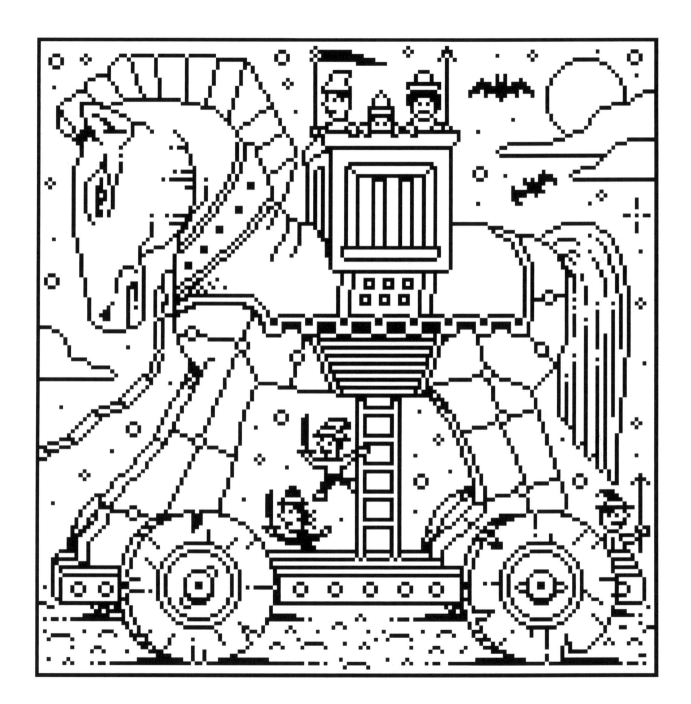

SEA SERPENTS

Ophidia sea serpents live primarily in the Eahta Sea which borders to the west of 8-bit Kingdom. The Ophidia serpents are gigantic water-dwelling monsters that, when surfacing to attack boats and ships, will tower terrifyingly over the ocean's surface. Many brave boatsmen have battled the Ophidia, but few have lived to tell the tale of the encounter.

Despite having wings, the Ophidia do not use them to fly. These wings are used as underwater flippers, allowing the large creatures to travel beneath the waves at speeds eight times faster than any royal ship. Their tiny arms are quite useless and at times comical, but the Ophidia are no laughing matter.

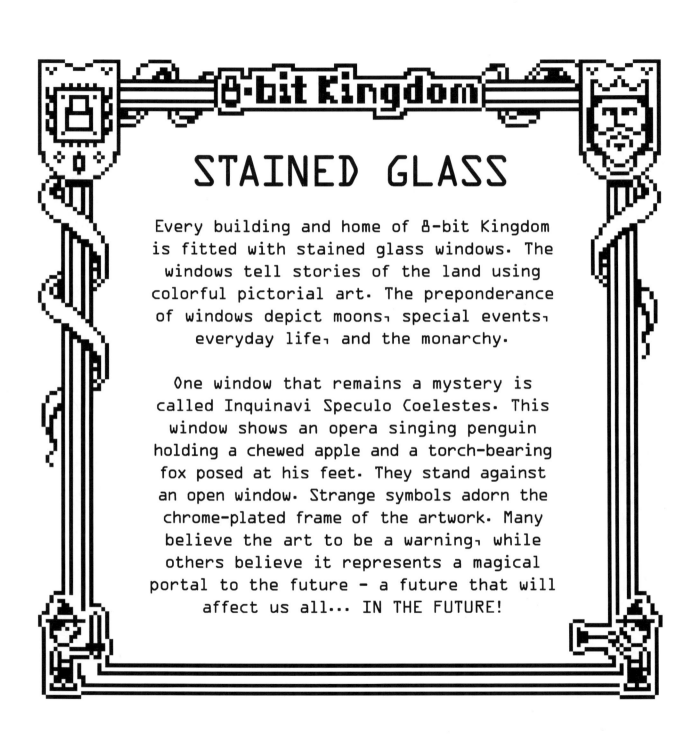

8-bit Kingdom

STAINED GLASS

Every building and home of 8-bit Kingdom is fitted with stained glass windows. The windows tell stories of the land using colorful pictorial art. The preponderance of windows depict moons, special events, everyday life, and the monarchy.

One window that remains a mystery is called Inquinavi Speculo Coelestes. This window shows an opera singing penguin holding a chewed apple and a torch-bearing fox posed at his feet. They stand against an open window. Strange symbols adorn the chrome-plated frame of the artwork. Many believe the art to be a warning, while others believe it represents a magical portal to the future - a future that will affect us all... IN THE FUTURE!

ABOUT THE AUTHOR

For ten years, Joe Lacey worked as a pixel artist and animator. His work can be seen in the Fisher-Price game cartridges for Pixter, which include Monster Shop and Dino Draw. He also created the art and animation for a number of casino-styled online video games and interactive educational apps.

In addition to digital games, Joe creates art for toys and books. Some of his publications include *Famous Illustrators of the Golden Age Coloring Portfolio* (Diner Mighty) and *Lyrics by Lennon & McCartney Coloring Songbook* (Crayola). He co-authored the award-nominated *The Musical Touch of Leonard Nimoy* with his wife Darlene.

Joe currently lives in Los Angeles, California and prefers movies without CGI. His favorite video game is Joust.

....

JoeLacey.com
joelaceyillustrator on Instagram and Facebook

If you enjoyed this book, let us know by posting a review or contacting us at:

info@dinermighty.com

If you colored these pages, share your images to social media with the hashtag:

#8bitkingdom

Want to know when new books are coming out? Follow us here:

facebook.com/DMGpublications
instagram.com/dinermighty

www.dinermighty.com

Publisher of humor and pop culture books.

Made in the USA
Middletown, DE
03 December 2021

54183154R00051